**ANCHOR BOOKS**

PROGRESSIVE THOUGHTS

Edited by

Heather Killingray

First published in Great Britain in 1999 by
ANCHOR BOOKS
Remus House, Coltsfoot Drive,
Woodston,
Peterborough, PE2 9JX
Telephone (01733) 898101

HB ISBN 1 85930 668 3
SB ISBN 1 85930 663 2

FOREWORD

Anchor Books is a small press, established in 1992, with the aim of promoting readable poetry to as wide an audience as possible.

We hope to establish an outlet for writers of poetry who may have struggled to see their work in print.

The poems presented here have been selected from many entries. Editing proved to be a difficult task and as the Editor, the final selection was mine.

I trust this selection will delight and please the authors and all those who enjoy reading poetry.

Heather Killingray
Editor

CONTENTS

COMPETITIVE

It takes about as long to understand
the way things operate, as the time left
to fail to alter them. We find one hand
too many has no trumps and we're bereft.
We watch them gather tricks with expert ease
and follow suit, as if by Divine Law;
under the table slip their secret fees,
whilst Dealer sits and smiles at our applause.
Now change the metaphor and see swept leaves
all cleared for them, the rough all trimmed to swathe
their fair way forward to official greens:
how can we lesser mortals match such play?
Once bunkered by impossibility,
we are supposed to caddie quietly!

David Goodall

THE REALISATION OF HOPE

The past seems dark and very bleak
And a happy future is what we seek.
But with all this pollution
Pain and woe,
This doesn't seem very likely.
Until we live in harmony,
Lose the guns, knives,
The hatred,
Realise we are all one,
That no one is better than their neighbour,
Skin colour is just that
And not a reason for fear,
Freedom of speech
Means talking, listening
And yes, sometimes compromising.
No one is perfect,
Everyone is flawed,
But if we can all work together,
Forget our differences,
Realise we are all a small part
Of everyone else's existence,
As they are to ours,
Then, and only then,
Will we have a community that is willing to save this world
And create a brighter future, of hope and happiness, for us all to hold.

Lindsey Brown

FIVE LITTLE BIRDIES

Five little birdies
Sitting in a tree
One fell down
And broke his knee.

Four little birdies,
Flying by the wire
One got too close
And caught on fire.

Three little birdies
Eating pigeon seed
One choked to death,
And now he's deed.

Two little birdies
Thought it was hot
One flew down to rest
And then it got shot.

One little birdie
Flying by the cat
It got ate
And that was that.

Emily Chapman (13)

COMMERCIAL BABYLON, HER PLACE OF ORIGIN, AND SPIRITISTIC END
(Rev 18 and 19:6)

Hallelujah! Babylon's trinity is falling,
And all at the same time!
World traders, and the religious 'harlot' are
Drunk with human blood, a deadly wine.

The strong angel is holding 'her' millstone
Aloft, to pitch swiftly into the sea,
No craftsman or traders will she ever find
Again, to obey her political harlotry;

For by her spiritisitic practices all
Nations were misled;
When her religious harlot daughters had
Weak souls fornicating in their 'sickbed'.

Prophets, holy ones, and others she
Slaughtered, are numbered among her dead.
The political 'beast' and 'false prophet'
Will soon be abyssed, then Our Lord will wed.

Then God's righteous rule of justice will
Surely begin!
And His anger 'upon the air' will affect
Contemptuous ones living in unbridled sin.

'Great hail', with every missile the weight
Of a talent have descended upon Babylon's men;
Who blaspheme God due to these plagues
So great, during the time of their end. Amen.

While we wait for Babylon's oppressive end,
And total destruction of her trinity,
Our hope is to live with the Father, the Son,
And the Holy Spirit, in Christian charity.

R Thomas

4

LOVE LIES BLEEDING

Is love not blind to material things?
Money and promotion outweigh.
Casual indifference can cause more harm,
That a passion that binds two to stay.
There are no substitutes for feelings,
Feelings that both must share.
It is not enough to pretend emotions,
Both hearts must equally care.
Like the rose, love lies bleeding,
Blossomed only to fade,
When parting is ever so easy,
Who knows what price will be paid.

Philip Warwick

CHRISTMAS

So, once again, we go to my aunt's place
To see many a familiar face.
Everyone's once again here,
We've made it through another year.
There are fears the future will be sad
But let us be glad.
That we're not so poor,
We're here once more.

Sunil Hiranandani

CHRISTMAS TIDINGS

Christmas is a very wondrous time,
When cards received from friends of mine
Portray snow-laden fir trees, glistening white,
And Three Wise Men following a star so bright.

The holly and the mistletoe
Twin symbols of this celebration;
The robin with breast orange-red
Contrasts with the snow and waits to be fed.

Stately churches with pealing bells,
Their choirs sing out in exultation,
As Christmas time is brought to mind
Casting a holy spell on all mankind.

The logs in the hearth flicker and flame
As we lift our eyes and proudly proclaim
The coming of God's Son, the Holy Babe
Born in a stable, the human race to save.

Given by God's Almighty Hand
Bringing peace and joy throughout the land,
His Grace flowing down to each heart and soul
His Love blessing everyone and making us whole.

Florence May Scott

JUBILEE 2000

Sing a song of power
which stifles so much life.
Lots of million have-nots
baked in putrid debt.
   When the truth was opened
   the poor began to snitch.
   Wasn't that a huge surprise
   to set before the rich?

Sing a song of justice
as lively as a flea.
Till those wicked payments
bake in *Jubilee*.
   When more people clamour
   top Governments will quake.
   Isn't theirs a shaky rule
   to set before fair stake?

Sing a song of hoping
let all the children free.
Round the world they echo:
'bake equality.'
   When false debts are cancelled
   more nations can stand tall.
   Isn't that a simple truth
   to set upon our stall?

Ruth I Johns

ROLE PLAY

Our love life is fading, it's sad but it's true
And I feel that I must take some action
So maybe some role play will spice up our lives
Tell me, please, what's your honest reaction?

Henry Eight, Anne Boleyn - oh, the visions I have
Be a beast, fling me down on the bed
But instead of *demanding* my skull be detached
Perhaps I could just *give* you a good head!

Anthony, Cleopatra. What fun we could have
Place your dagger just within my grasp
Remove each others' togas in passionate haste
Run your frantic hands over may asp!

Captain Smith, Pocahontas. We'll sail the high seas
I'll be servile and you can pull rank
Demand that I do anything that you please
Like sit astride, 'stead of walking, your plank!

Like Maria and Tony (the Jets and the Sharks)
Our forbidden love could cause reaction
I'll be a Harrier (good for a jump)
And you show me your hammerhead action!

So I'll let you decide from what's listed above
Think about it whilst falling asleep
It's not that I'm kinky, but just one last thought
What say you be the farmer and I'll be the sheep?

Baa!

Karen Redmond-Smith

LIFE

Life is all about chance and we only get one try,
Many do well, while others struggle by.
Good things happen and bad things too
But whether it's nice or not there's nothing you can do.
As life can be kind or life can be bad
But we must appreciate it, as some lives are sad.
As everyone gets at least one bad card
And this can make life seem very hard.
But with all the bad there is hope
As we all learn how to cope.
With life's little troubles and growing pains
And from these experiences we do gain
A knowledge and understanding about what to do.
When things happen out of the blue
But life is not all doom and gloom
It gives you a freedom to explore different rooms
As life is precious so you should make the most of it.
Otherwise it'll end up *sh*t!*

Nichola Wells

ODE TO A CAT

Before the temples of Bubastis sank beneath the Egyptian sands
The grimalkin found its Eden at the hearths of man
Adored as dark angels by the acolytes of the sphinx
Moon-blessed the ruled until the last pharaoh fell
Then carried to Rome fell asleep at Liberty's feet
Until the winds of war drove them upon Albion's shore.

Still the scions of Bast stalk their prey upon our streets
When the lights are low and all our ways abandoned
A golden scintilla seen within an adamantine eye
Betrays the secret of their uncanny presence
Sliding betwixt argent shafts of lucent moonlight
Prowling our properties in search of slow kills.

In the shadows Protean forms shape shift and pass
As silent upon concrete as a cat's paw upon the waves
The sybarite deceptions of the day are torn away
As primal fires rage in the soul of the shade
Until the dark lords of an old order arise anew
Piercing the night like bolts of black lightning.

At midnight our screaming familiars form into covens
Where wanton whores inflame frenzies of flesh
Abandoning their bodies to any brutal lover
That dares give battle to fill their bellies with life
Then hissing with delight as the barbs draw blood
Galenthias abases herself in worship of Hecate.

Dawn drives the diabolic shameless to our doors
Whilst votive in their pagan jaws are broken wings
To be lain before the altar of our sanctum arms
And offered as bribes to avert our prying eyes
Then drifting into dreams they twitch crimson lips
Until night beats anew, the dark drums of their secret lusts.

Lee John Barnes

REVENGE

Although you are my brother.
That's the fault of our mother.
She didn't want you born.
So you were always treated with scorn.
They said you were a fool.
Every day at school.
Yet I was thought the best.
Always above the rest.
I passed all of my exams.
While you got involved in scams.
My future lay in the stars.
And you were stealing cars.
When you were first sent inside.
We tried our best to hide.
The fact that you were kith and kin.
Hoping someone would do you in.
You couldn't even find a girl.
Then we found out about your world.
Of men and whips and chains.
And enjoying each other's pain.
So you can't bear a grudge.
Now that I'm a judge.
I'll never understand.
Why you had to kill a man.
Because he wouldn't play along.
Does that really make him wrong?
So it's with a satisfying breath.
I sentence you to death.

Trevor Foster

BLUE SKIES

Blue skies remain
a therapy I am holding
a flower in my hand
watching nature day by day
A beam of sun in the light
opens on a conscience mind
The garden becomes my spring
The sea, near at hand
resting those motives
calm and tranquil
inducing a certain
ceremony of performed
ritual the fall of waves
A season in change
dark by night -
with its secrecy
of opened challenge
to the stars and universe.

Roger Thornton

CARNATION

Oh you were always everywhere
Helping those for who you cared
Living your life for everyone else,
Never worrying about yourself.
Travelling places far and wide.
Leaving early and returning tired.
Never stopping to have a rest
Working your hardest to achieve the best.
And this is why you were loved so much
For happiness you brought with your touch,
And even though you are gone
The love you gave is still as strong,
And this is why a carnation I wear
To say thank you and show that I care.

Sarah Louise Morris

THE WILLOW'S LAMENT TO HER RIVER
(Re flood prevention of River Tay)

Though tears fell
Hushed in stillness
Roots caved in on
Mother earth
What is it happens
To our river
She wailed with loud
Momentous course
'Twas this - her birthright given
Unconditionally with love
Served friends of stream
To mimicry - for
Their destined time -
Disturbed.
In bond alone together
Pertaining to the sense of touch
Each sighed a lasting
fond adieu
To a river - prized so much.

Irene Gunnion

Sammy Squirrel

I like a bit of peace and comfort in the cold, dreary, icy months.
It's not much fun stuck up a tree as the growling winter grunts.
I suppose it would be beneficial to seek a warmer, cosier home.
So I'll don my thick, furry winter jacket and set off far to roam.

I think I'll visit a human tree when the owners take their leave.
I'll just play Santa coming down the chimney never to deceive.
The car has gone, all lights are out, so scrambling down I'll go.
It's sooty in the darkness as I curl on a fleecy rug's soft snow!

My tree is fine, the core containing, copious canopies of wood.
A wealth of opportunity for sharpening teeth to lift my mood!
I'll just hop over shelves of ornaments, tossing them with pride.
Off skid old china figurines, fragmenting along the floor aside!

Curtains are in for a ripping time as I scramble above or below.
I can't really help it; sturdy ledges are needed for a swift flow.
Oops, sorry about the settees, as silky cushions split open wide!
I really need to have somewhere warm where I may safely hide.

I'll sharpen my teeth on table legs, rattle melodies on the piano.
Rich notes taste of purest ivory better than that squishy banana.
I fear carved faces above the fireside, so on the noses I'll gnaw.
Old canvases offer feeble support as I extricate my eagle claw!

A human sneaks in the door so I must scurry to enter a fast race!
He's chasing me round the room, everything tumbling in his face.
The din increases as he catches me, sprinting wildly for the door.
My apologies to poor owners, as insurers this debacle just ignore!

T Burke

OUR LIVES

Whatever, is it all about,
We will never really know.
We are put here for a lifetime,
And then we have to go.

Whatever, we can make of it
Then, it's truly up to us
Some people take it in their stride,
But some, just make a fuss.

Some don't know, 'what they're here for'
And make everybody sad,
But right from the beginning,
They wish they never had!

E B Holcombe

SEPTEMBER

Your face is rain,
I slip into my raincoat
with all the burned
ribbons of summer,
Your love hangs down
into wet trees,
you come from the sky
with a dusty kind
of loneliness,
a stranger walking
me into autumn.

Marion Schoeberlein

VICTORIAN ARCADE

Just off the teaming thousands
Up a side street on the right,
Waits a quiet cavern
With a dim and cooling light.

Step inside the archway
To the patterns on the floor,
Tiled in subtle colours.
Feel the polished wooden doors.

See the potted palm trees
And the iron balustrades,
Painted in the colours
Of their glorious heydays.

Take your eyes up to the roof,
Three stories round a square.
And climb the bare stone steps to find
The quaint shops selling there.

Small antiques and crafty things,
But quality as well;
Artists needs and herbalists,
Fine china and glass bells.

A wholefood place where you can eat,
With wedding cakes in rows.
An old bookshop where you can browse.
A shop for 'different' clothes.

Pottering shops if you have the time.
Specialist shops of taste.
Step through the arch to a different world,
Away from the rush and haste.

Jean Armitage

PAN

The intake of splendour injects forward motion
And the feeling of Pan is arcane
But the Pan I perceive with remoteness and fear
When the crags steal the light from the glen
The few seconds it takes develops or breaks
The character expected of man
The lustre of rock when sombre and stark
Can startle if you come upon Pan.

What manner of bestowal is our fear of the dark
Is it deity superstition or ignorance
And will we bestow like our kith and kin
Or help them enjoy and enhance
No horns, no ears, no legs of a goat
Will darkness bring or feign
The light once directed is now reflected
But the splendour beneath stays the same

But Pan as in Greek myth for those unbeknownst
Don't need veil of darkness to call
From ascent or direct to descent or reflect
The feeling of Pan can befall
This God of flocks and of shepherds
Who invented the musical pipe
Was it the sound of the breeze that inspired him
Or is myth vindication of fright.

Pòl Mac

LISTENING

Lying in bed, a-listening to the gathering storm,
Under a blanket, a pillow for my head, nice and warm,
Thinking of the roaring wind and the pouring rain
Battering on the windows, gurgling down the drain.

The wind coming from nowhere to nowhere in such a hurry,
Bringing down the leaves, making clouds a-scurry.
Telling us that summer's gone, that winter's on its way,
Say goodbye to the sunshine, hello to skies of grey.

Thinking of those people, their duty must not shirk,
Out in all this weather on their way to work.
Of the animals, no roof above for them,
Of flowers being torn away from stem.

Of foxes and of badgers, out foraging for food,
Can't stay at home, must feed the hungry brood.
Of owls out hunting, cannot hear their prey,
Must hunt tonight, cannot wait for day.

Of horses and of cattle, way out upon the moor,
Not for them the shelter of byre or stable door,
Nor tents or wellingtons or waterproof,
Just soaking backs and muddy hoof.

Ain't arf glad I'm 'uman, ain't you?

J H Vincent

YESTERYEAR OR TOMORROW?

By just staring quietly into space
One's mind can drift back, picturing bygone years.
Of when the old appeared, to the young, all lavender and lace
Of when the young seemed contented with few problems or fears.

But time and memory readily enhances the past
For life then, for many, was not a bed of roses
Large sectors of mankind to traumas quite vast
Were subjected, to wars and hardship. What else one supposes?

The older generations call them the good old days
And it's easy to see why they think themselves right
For despite so called progress, there's still a lack of grays
In a world needing to be more than just black or white.

There are rules for that and laws for this
And bureaucracy hovers over much we hold dear
In an ideal world we would certainly not miss
The many aspects of evil which cause hate and fear.

In the good old days, the world seemed a vast place
But as each day dawns it appears to diminish
For speed of travel is increasing at an astronomical pace
And life is becoming frantic - where, when will it finish?

It couldn't have been God's intention that life should be this way
With such extreme contrasts in the lives of the populace
There are far too many nations in the world today
Who have to fight to survive and gross indignities face.

Which brings most satisfaction - to look back or forward
The future is unknown and the past is dead and gone
But whichever we do, there will always be that cord
That links the future to the past, to what's been lost and won.

Ros Silom

FICKLE TIME

So, this is where fickle time has brought me,
To the brink, the wintertime of my life.
What must I expect? Slow senility?
Waning intellect? Forgetfulness rife?
Saddened, I gaze down at my thickened limbs
And I remember how they used to be,
Sheathed in the sheerest silk, shapely and slim.
Joints that didn't click, so painless, so free,
With dainty feet, tucked into high-heeled shoes . . .
But I have no power to hold back time,
Nor would I, if I were able to choose.
Though my life has been fruitfully sublime
I know that my earthly span ends, in truth,
To clear the path for shining springtime youth.

Valerie McKinley

A Woman's Lot

I wish I was rich, I don't care what anyone thinks,
I'm sick of *do-gooders* who say money stinks.
I plod to the factory every evening at five
And work like a dog just to survive.
What a life full of tiredness and despair,
As I greet my loved ones as they pass on the stair.
They're coming in as I'm going out,
Is this really what family life's all about?
There are millions like me, we have no choice,
And nobody cares, or hears our voice.
So when folk not short of a bob or two
Try to tell us what we really should do
I could spit in their eye, and try not to cry.
Maybe one day, it'll be my turn to fly.

June V Johnson

THE REPENTING

Upon the wilderness of truth,
under storm clouds of proof,
rummaging for liberty.
Washed by the whispering wind,
still this twisted tongue has sinned
with the leverage of purity.

Unburden this tortured soul,
unfurl the gaping hole
and quell my animosity.
Now on the anvil of tomorrow,
I must rejuvenate from sorrow,
as once again I relate to dignity.

J R Griffiths

LAURENTIAN STREAM

Come to this dear Laurentian scene,
Where starts a tiny bubbling stream,
At which the frog and I may drink,
Where partridge dart, by the mountains' brink.
For a while we hear no trickle,
Streams you know are very fickle.
Searching, soon we hear her laughing,
As over the stones, she stumbles splashing
Fishes fall beneath her spell,
The bank has formed her a wishing well.
On she glides as if her fate
The end of a journey does await,
Swept past shady bowing trees,
Where blends the music of birds and bees.
A ballet of butterflies dance and skip
Sleepy cattle stoop to sip.
Then below the tree bark bridges,
Winds the stream around the ridges,
She has come to join the river,
Arm in arm they flow together.
Weep not, nor be too much forlorn,
Because of this a sea is born.

Clara Ward Marshall

ACHERON'S SAIL

His mist has settled, thin
Across the Styx, rows her bloodless into the rustling thickets
Imbedded rich into his paled cloak of Lysol
She awakens

Charon, with his unforboding hood
Bribed his godless toll unto the weeping mossy bank
Her black art bruised, black hearted
Reciting her heathen prayer
As if like a Kaddish

The pitch has whistled me dark
I scratch the scab
It soon bleeds into an embroidered necessity
That congeals, thickening softly into gentle moon-flowers
As her perfected calyx lies still

I am the permafrost, the kamikaze one
The carrion-flower
Immersed into the dark water, myself drowned pure

I gave birth the beast, the bitch
With it's amphibian scales, its deathly groan
That writhes in hydra pits, writhing of its own accord
We are sixty-times dovetailed into stone
We are both immortal

Yet we eat like worms
Navigating themselves sheepishly from the terrified earth
Sucking rain droplets beneath the Reaper's ever-failing harvest

For once her pulse falls silent
It is merely dormant, she lies inattentive
As Lucifer treads the soil with incessant black hooves
She creeps along the gentle toes.

Ian Patrick Wright

REFLECTING SYMMETRY

What does it reflect,
the bedroom mirror?
- The symmetrical moons
of your breasts,
and the perfect cleft
of your buttocks,
as you undress -
each curved thigh
a soft mirror to the other,
convexities
and concavities of flesh
leave me spellbound.

Sometimes your striptease
teases me erect,
but tonight,
fatigued,
I bury my face in my pillow -
symmetrically we sink into sleep,
and the body of the bed
swallow us,
whole.

Marc Harris

SELF ABUSE

H, three lines, two vertical, one horizontal.
My naked arm bleeds not.
No blood, no pain.
Depression runs as deep as the scars which mark
my naked body.
Dreams disappear into memories that fade into
the sickness of humanity.

E, one vertical, three horizontal
Still no blood, still no pain
The phone Doesn't ring. No knocks at the door
No postcards wishing I was there.

L, one vertical, one horizontal.
Two lines only.
That's good, I'm feeling weak.
H and E start to bleed.
A single tear falls silently on to the E, fills with
Blood and races across into the H.

A strange letter marks the end.
One vertical line and half a circle.
My arm is now a red mess filled with regret.
A darkness falls. I can no longer see.

Help!

Simon Flawn

ONE IN FIVE WOMEN . . .

Panic-stricken, she prepares the evening meal
and vacuums for the second time that day.
Frantic actions suggesting the imminent arrival of a special visitor.
She looks at the clock in horror - only 3 minutes left!

'I'm home!' Her heart pounds and her stomach churns.
'Why is the house such a mess?'
'Why isn't dinner ready?'
' . . . What have you been doing all day!'

She stutters over her words, trying to account for each minute.
He checks the supermarket receipt
and questions her on her reason for buying sanitary towels.
'. . . give me the cash . . . they're not for me . . . I'm not paying!'

'Hang on . . . ! You left Safeway at 10:28,
what did you do until 11.05 . . .? Why?'
She'd collected library books to help with her job.
'Pathetic! Why don't you get a *proper* job?'

Bravely, she tries to defend herself
explaining that she's a housewife and mother too.
'Huh, you're useless at both of those!'
She feels the anger and sadness well up inside her.

'Any post?'
She hands him the phone bill - unopened - itemised, of course.
With a highlighter pen he carefully marks her calls.
' . . .Why did you phone them . . . Who's this? - I'm not paying . . . !'

Just time for today's ironing, she thinks.
'Make sure you don't mark that . . . Crease those properly!'
He puts a video on for the children.
'Let's have sex you frigid bitch,' he pants.

As she is raped she thinks of all the other women
who are abused and too *pathetic* to fight back . . .

Linda Rose

I Know a Mary 'That Is Quite Contrary'

A Mary that loves to feel the breeze
Whistling around her knees.

Standing wherever it appears
On cliff tops so high that nearly reach the sky.

Or on Piers and that she cannot deny
Heaven knows why, Maybe because she is shy

Although it cannot be said that she is not all there
I know that to be true, as I was also there
And someday we will do that again I know
You may think we are Mad
But I do not think that is so Bad

Paul Volante

POETRY BY CANDLELIGHT

The ray of hope in the darkness appears,
Illuminating each word that I write.
Banishing the nightfall, the demons, and fears . . .
Poetry, by candlelight.

Fiery images break through imagination,
Dancing in the cold, dim room.
Taking on shapes, a witch's formation,
And adding effervescence to the gloom.

The page looks alive, reflections slowly narrow,
Flickering, wax dripping, relief through the night.
The wall of boredom, blanketed now by shadow . . .
Poetry, by candlelight.

Kimberley Huggens

THE SANTA CLAUS

He sat on the cold wet pavement huddled on an island of blanket
Amidst the swirling sea of Christmas shoppers.
In the centre of his island, he held safely his dog, whose devoted expression
Gazed upon his carer with immense love.
I walked passed with footsteps sounding hollow to my ears.
Then, retracing my steps, entered the shop full of presents for pampered pets.
Three bone-shaped chocolate covered biscuits
And mixed assorted shapes of different colours cost only 55p.

I mustn't touch him I thought, neither did I want to upset him.
Stopping in front of him, I nervously asked would he be offended
If I offered him biscuits for his dog.
With sad expression he shook his head in acceptance. As my eyes met his
I knew I would not forget him.
Handing him the bag, I felt guilty I had not bought more.
'All the best,' I said. To me, it sounded pathetic but it was the best I could do.
Unexpectedly I smiled at the sad young face turned toward me.
He smiled back, the smile lighting up his face and reflecting the warmth that flowed
Within that island in the midst of the uncaring sea. A tidal wave of impact
Floated inside my head.

I wondered if he guessed the aloneness I felt as I hurried home to myself that Christmas Eve.
For less than a fraction of a second, a glance met. Souls touched.
Barely. But to be held in Eternity.
Maybe I had met him before in another Lifetime. Maybe I will meet him again.

I had made sure not to touch his hand. Yet he had touched my heart.
For it could have been me on the cold wet pavement. For a brief
moment - it was.
If you think, it could have been you.

I'll write this poem, I said to myself. Only I could find no poetry to
express this encounter.
But strengthened was a desire to try and be of help to all Beings in the
Universe.

This was the gift he gave. For only 55p worth of biscuits for his dog.

M Riches

AGE WITHOUT FEAR

An ancient relic that's how I feel,
Wobbly limbs with no appeal,
All I can do is observe,
My time nearly now served.

The deterioration is steady,
Yet in myself I am ready,
This untidy bundle to leave,
Of pipes and bones that's me.

Yet I suffer not,
Any specific ailment, it's the lot,
That is simply wearing out,
And I will not be long about.

Does this knowledge make me sad?
Do I wish back to be as a lad?
I do not think so,
I am not frightened to go.

With truthful calm and tranquillity,
I accept the inevitability,
Of my years with no fear,
And even impatience not to be here.

My memory is not too bad,
Though concentration I do not have,
Yet I recall with remarkable clarity,
All those wonderful memories,
The times and places I did see,
That led me to the old age of 83.

Herbert Newton

UNDERSTANDING THOUGHTS!

Dear One that dwells above the earth - I have received from your mighty hands this very day of life, untold wealth, I have the endless beauty of the skies, forever changing day after day. I have the wonders of your earth no matter where I choose to gaze, and should I gain all the kingdoms of this world, they in themselves could never replace the untold wealth that you allow the hand of mother nature to bring and I am blessed indeed to understand - it is by the powers of your mighty ways - skies , sea and earth are all part of your creative works and should I ever have any doubts, let them be about myself, and still give You above the full glory you deserve for all your creative works of art before my gift of sight - this very day of life.

Amen.

Rowland Patrick Scannell

DEATH BY DRUGS

He has no expression,
his eyes are glazed.
He's been taking drugs,
well, it's all the craze!
Doesn't know where he's at,
or where he's been.
He's not really bothered,
if he's been seen.

His parents don't know,
what he does out of sight.
If they saw him now,
they'd get such a fright.
He looks like a ghost,
the living dead.
He doesn't understand,
what's being said.

He has to steal,
so he can pay,
for the drugs he needs
throughout the day.
Can't manage without them,
needs more and more,
until one day
he hits the floor.

He's dying now,
but doesn't care.
Can't feel a thing,
his eyes just stare.
His mates gather round,
and kneel by his side.
Desperate to help him,
too late! he died.

Barbara Kiss

HOPE FROM DESPAIR

Bare with no adornment
They reach up to the sky,
It greets them not.
No acknowledgement that they're there,
Grey skeletons in a grey background
No excitement, nothing.

But, come the spring
The feathery brushstrokes
Erupt into green.
Those limbs once playing dead
Transform into a thing of beauty
A tree,
Enhanced in a sky of blue
Saying, 'Hi, I'm alive.'

Lydia J Thomas

IMAGES

The mirror reflects an image
That image it is me
Writing words down on a page
The things you cannot see
The times I've hurt, the times I've cried
The times I've had a fall
These are kept deep down inside
A smile just hides them all
But for every tear I've ever cried
A lesson has been learned
No more tears my face has dried
My knowledge was hard earned
But now I know I'll never fall down
And I'll never run a mile
I can wipe away a worry or frown
With a genuine smile
When I look back I don't regret
The mistakes that I have made
'Cause I know I've kept myself respect
And the heartaches they do fade
Now looking in the mirror
Looking back at me
I'm happy with my image
And I'm happy back at me.

Wendy Carrier

THE MAYOR

The mayor is a councillor elected to act
As first citizen, he certainly does that
His stage is the borough in which he is mayor
His clothes are of animal fur, but he doesn't care
That some poor creature had to die
To make him look special and feel high
His chain is of gold but it means nothing
That someone mined it so it could be given to him
He has a limo but makes no admission
It's causing global warming via carbon emissions
Instead of that and all of the fuss
Why doesn't he use a pushbike or get on a bus?
He could stop wearing fur and stick to suit and tie
Then less creatures would die
He could go to less parties for free and pretend
But why doesn't he look at the sharp end?
The homeless who live in boxes on the street
The sick and the elderly in need - it's them he should meet
Stop acting like a stuck-up fool
Face the people in need, they don't have it so cool.

P Edwards

THE POOR LITTLE ELEPHANT

Poor little elephant,
Alone from dawn to dusk.
The only reason you still live,
Is because you have no tusks.
Once the ground would tremble,
As your mighty herds came by,
But pollution, poachers, and the ivory trade,
Caused your kind to slowly die.
So blow your trumpet loud and long,
And hope another herd will hear,
But they've burned your forests and ploughed your fields,
So there are no others near.
Alone you walk that final mile,
And forget about that fear,
Into the elephants' graveyard,
Because you know the end is near.

Jay Berkowitz

SWEET THREE DAY FOREST

It was one of those rare frosty mornings
for the third day in a row
the fields were dusted with icing sugar
and tomorrow's forecast was snow

tankers and spreaders were out in force
for the ground could now carry their weight
and soon the sugar frosting
was covered with chocolate

the aroma in deep freeze suspended
was anything but fragrant
many a nostril was offended
washing lines remained vacant

on the fourth day came the snow
then rain to make despondent
soon the hardened frosty fields
became as soft as fondant

oh those mint cool memories
of frost that lasted weeks not days
when life went at a slower pace
to prevent today skidding into tomorrow

Heather Kirkpatrick

To A Painting

This quiet place where early in the morn
The gentle mist will rise,
Life stirs once more at dawn
As winged ones soar upwards to the skies.
This quiet place where silver birches tall
Stand swaying in the breeze,
Red deer across the valley call,
Wild creatures shelter near the trees.
The paling stars look down into the dell
All clad in autumn gold,
These lovely hills I know so well
Inspire my memories to unfold.

Sylvia Taggart

MORNING FAIR

In the freshness of this early morn
People still sleep.
At its acute angle from the east,
The sun shines from an untouched sky.
The slumberers, clinging to their beds,
Miss the crispness of this newborn day.
Nestled between their covers,
They do not witness
The quiet solemnity of the morn.
Dew hangs heavily on blade and leaf,
Soon to be lapped up by the ascending sun,
Leaving flowers and trees to bask and wilt
In summer glory!
At this pre-waking hour
An eerie emptiness fills the streets,
Recently unwrapped from darkness.
The only sound from birds, long up,
Chorusing in surrounding docile trees.
In these dawning, unused hours,
Everything is yet unspoilt.
A hushed expectancy hangs
In the promise of a wonderful day!

Pat Heppel

ROYALTY

I don't like Royalty not one little bit,
Especially when on their thrones they sit.
I'd pension them off if I had my way,
Alas no one listens to what I have to say.
I'm just one of the poor sods who pays their wages,
To keep them in big houses and waited on by pages.
I fail to see what good they really are,
I would have them pickled and put in jars.

Don Goodwin

TREASURED COMPANIONS

She sits alone in her cosy home:
Loved ones are now away,
Inanimate objects are the friends,
She tends with love each day.

Her keepsakes seem to sparkle and gleam,
Brought from many a place,
Bringing a smile for a little while,
Creasing the wrinkled face.

By a quirk of fate, a china plate,
Some silver and some brass,
Seem doubly dear: they are bringing near
Fond echoes of the past.

Each precious treasure, giving pleasure,
To her they seem to speak
Of the days long past, but oh, alas!
A silence they must keep.

The warmth they exude is doing good,
They're worth their weight in gold,
But come the day when she fades away,
'They'll sell for gold' I'm told.

Margaret Knox Stubbs

SEEING STARS

Europe, dazed and seeing stars
Is dealt a mighty blow
As corrupt officials sigh relief
They'll not be forced to go

Fraudsters who have proved their worth
Integrity displayed
A warning to all Europeans
Noisily conveyed

A commission run by criminals
That people cannot trust
Which is meteing out its orders still
Is monstrously unjust

A parliament of parasites
A complement of crooks
Hanging onto power
By their sharp, yet dirty hooks

Kim Montia

ALL OF THEM

In the way of life
They are poor saps
Who will see all
That ill done again
No to them all
No to all of them
The way they live
Each day is a
Hard existence yet live
They all will do
If it suits them
As well as others
Ugly, angry, poor saps
Want ugly, mad darkness
To sweep over us
No to all of them
They are so alone
So lost, so finished
Yet they are out
Of touch with all
In the one society
They just live in
If they live then
They must have sense
And not ignore others
The bad sorry others
Are worlds apart from
Us right now and
You always see it
You see it all
In that one way.

Richard Clewlow

ICO Global Challenger

Richard Branson flew up in the air
In his big balloon, with blue eyes and blonde hair!

With red flames a flaming
And balloon now enlarging!

Up they went full of anticipation and excitement
Hoping the balloon would never be rent!

Starting from Marrakesh in Morocco:
Then through a 'corridor' between Iran and Russia
Over Pakistan, Nepal and India
Between Everest and K² in the Himalayas
To China who rescinded permission; which caused them to slow down!
Then to the Tibetan plateau!

So Steve Fosset, Per Lindstrom and Richard Branson
Had to change course to avoid Iraq and wait for
China's decision; losing time and fuel!

Beaten by a fierce trough of low pressure the balloon
Bounced across the Pacific Ocean like a toy balloon!
They landed in Honolulu on Christmas day 1998!

8 days of bliss!

Just envisage this!

Marie Barker

CHILDREN PIE

Ingredients:

One large grass meadow
Half a dozen children
Two or three small dogs
- According to taste
Some pebbles
Few drops of brook
Few flower sprays.

Mix the children and dogs together
- Round among the purple heather
Place them in the meadow
- Stirring constantly
Just for mischief
- Add a climbing tree
Pour the brook over the pebbles
- Add one or two water devils
Sprinkle the meadow with the flowers
- Let them catch the April showers
Spread overall a deep blue sky
- And there you have 'Children Pie'
Bake in the hot sunshine
- Just ten minutes at a time
When well browned, remove to bath tub
- Allow to cool, then rub.

Barbara Sherlow

ANGRY

I am angry
I am mad
I am annoyed
I am bad

I am stupid
I am silly
I am annoyed
I'm a silly billy

Daisy Gammon *(8)*

LOST INNOCENCE

A child was I, white empty, virgin page,
Awaiting the pens that there would write
The man: and, having writ, would light the stage
On which I played 'til death's long night.

They whole world was mine, and all it gave
I only saw with curious delight.
I knew no laws, nor saw life ended in a grave:
Love shielded me from any form of fright.

Love followed sleep of the unprinted mind,
Rich in refreshment for the day's unending joys,
When all the things around me were combined
Into the shape of ever pleasing toys.

A cot was the world, and then a vastly room,
And soon a garden and a hedge and gates,
When trees were my horizon, and the coloured bloom,
The loveliest toy of all, my exploring finger waits.

Alas! Impermanency took my joys away:
And innocence, that wanted nothing but the hour.
Soon I owned 'things': soon I must spend to play:
Soon I must work to spend: soon I must seek my power.

And oh! that power irks me to control
The half taught mind, the undiscipline of tongue.
Why want the knowledge of man's worldly role,
When by its sight, the caring heart is wrung?

Rannoch Melville Russell

EVENSONG

Dusk drifts into the garden
Now the blackbird's solo starts
The Priory starts church bell practice
Will it lift up our hearts?
His anthem begins on a low key
Then higher the notes slowly rise
An upward thrust through the pale black sky
Me thinks they'll reach Paradise
Church bells swing join the blackbird's hymn
A duet is born and then
In rapture they blend, one evensong
      Alleluia and Amen.

Barbara Robson

The Sinking Of The Titanic

She was named the ship of dreams,
they called her unsinkable or so it seems,
but in April came an unusual sight,
when an iceberg struck that fateful night.

That ship was so big and was sure to go down,
even the designer upon his face wore a frown,
the iceberg struck and punched a hole,
and he knew there was not enough lifeboats to save every soul.

Now all they could do is sit and wait,
of what would be dealt by the cruel hand of fate,
the moans and groans as the ship starts to sink,
people falling to their deaths, no one had a chance to stop to think.

The ship is slowly vanishing, almost gone,
someone fouled up, it was all done wrong,
people falling into the cold cruel sea,
not knowing what their fate was to be.

The screams of torment could be heard that night,
as the Titanic sank to her death out of sight,
hundreds of people in the freezing cold waves,
laying there in their watery graves.

Women and children even died that night,
it was so horrific and a terrible sight,
but now it's just history that's so true,
how many lives were saved, too little, so very few.

Louisa Sarah Jane Wilson

BLUE SAPPHIRE AND GREEN EMERALD

When sunshine dapples through the leaves,
On bluebells massed, beneath the trees,
   Of green beech bursting, springtime kissed,
   Trunks wreathed in early morning mist.
A sea unending, hazy blue,
Into a distant fading hue,
   Each single flower a perfect gem,
   Blue sapphire, on green emerald stem.
As daytime warms, the mists retreat,
Cast diamond dewdrops, at our feet,
   To shimmer, glimmer, sparkle bright,
   We shield our eyes to see the sight.
Oh what a vision, beauty seen,
Majestic beeches, rise supreme,
   Above the blue, they cast a shade,
   Protecting glen and leafy glade.
Hear the silence, feel the peace,
Taste sweet air, let cares release.
   This must be heaven right here on earth,
   Where mother nature's giving birth.

James W Sargant

WHITE

White snowflakes floating in the ground
High in the air whirling round and round
Icicles melting to the ground
Taking lots of time
Every day, to melt away.

Daniel O Rustage (9)

EMOTIONS OF A CHILD

E   ach new dawning day, while a child's at play, laughter
   or sadness may be felt.

M   aking their hearts beat fast or slow depending how
   the cards that day are dealt.

O   nes innermost feelings be it joy or sadness is oft-times
   hidden from view.

T   he child's facial expression cannot hide their feelings,
   one glance tells what they're going through.

I   n this world where hunger, poverty and sickness exist,
   causing many a tearful eye.

O   ne must help those less fortunate children, remember.
   'There but for the grace of God go I'.

N   ow a long time ago Ten Commandments on stone
   tablets were given to show us the way.

S   o instil their teaching in our children and they'll
   make a peaceful world some day.

James McBride

OLIVIA IN THE GARDEN
(So nice to see Olivia)

Olivia in the moonlight like a flower,
It's springtime, so nice to see Olivia
In the garden among the flowers pottering.

Summertime comes now with Olivia on holiday
Enjoying herself abroad
Still with flowers and in the sun;
So nice to see Olivia
Dancing in the moonlight
Among friends.

K A Shepherd

THE FIRST DECILLENNIUM

Ten years makes a decade
Ten decades makes a century
Ten centuries makes a millennium
So ten millennia make a decillennium, see.

I am the Atlanticity
20,000 feet beneath the sea
On December 31st 9999
Leaving the first decillennium AD.

I have come here by transatlantic subway train
Travelling at 9,000 mph, or more
I'm halfway between London and New York
In a domed city of 60 levels 1,000 miles from shore.

I am getting ready to celebrate
The start of 10,000, the second decillennium
At midnight I will dance with glee.

The clocks now strike twelve midnight
10,000 AD has begun
A new decillennium is dawning
Lots of technology and fun!

H G Griffiths

No Ideality

You can't choose your paternal pair
You could be born into going nowhere
There may as well be no air
If life is unfair
If you develop disease
More serious than a sneeze
It could be that the thorn
Depends on the place you were born

The Arabs have their desert
The Sudanese have their dirt
Cockneys have their crimes
And the Welsh have their mines

We can't choose who we are
Not many of us become a star
Or go all that far
Most of us have a limited repertoire

This is due to our stifling surroundings
Which leads to our undoings
Through lack of adequate earnings
A lot of us stop our breathings.

You don't have a choice of nationality
All you can understand is your own reality
Dishing out poverty is man's speciality
But unfortunately equality is an impracticality
As there is no ideality.

Tay Collicutt

BORN AT THE WRONG TIME - BOSNIA, NOV '92

A child is born into a war
Nothing can erase what her poor eyes saw
Death and destruction in her first years of life
Losing friends and family happens so rife
Just take her hand and lead her away
So she can return to the peace she hopes for one day
But when she returns nothing is the same
No family to reach out and call her name
Life will have to start again for this lost soul
To bring up her child in peace is her only goal.

Phill Minns

BONNIE

My name is Bonnie, a former dray horse,
Yet my brother Ronnie serves in the police force.
When my owner retired from the daily round, it created a problem,
What could the solution be? It was so difficult, what to do with me.
For to relate the truth, gone was my youth. I'm now quite long in the
tooth. What would my future be? Certainly a problem, to face for me,
no chance of entering the chase to jump or to race at Aintree.

It's a puzzle to exercise the mind, for no work of any kind could we
find. We are not at all work dodging, but there must be a way we may
pay for our board and lodging! When I was of the age, with youth on
my side, I could always furnish a pony ride, but for my future, no one
did provide.

There was no mention of the old horses' pension for the horses as no
one applied, the concern is about my future security it is then that one
finds, that humans are kind for I can now see how I can be content, with
their money well spent on providing a horse sanctuary.

For even when I reach my end, may I rival the dog to become man's
best friend? For me there's no longer to be any worry or wondering,
I'm being adopted by the Red Wing!

Benny H Howell

FACE OF FORTUNE

When all the clouds achieved a wispy look
And thunderheads were knocked into the womb
God gave me fortune, not in gold -
Fast friends and family,
A precious few.
Oh Sweet Rememberer, who knew my name,
And softly sang it like a quodlibet,
You made me feel that I was truly blessed.
And now, each morning when the sun appears
I tell myself you're here,
And so am I.

Carolyn Long

DON'T ASK!

He asked me to write,
But how can I write, my mind's blank?

I try to think,
But my mind wanders to other things.

I think of how I need my bed.

I look at my sheet
It's blank;
Like the inside of my head.

If you read this,
Then please remember,
Don't ask me to write
At this unholy hour.

Gerard Moore

BEAUTY

Beauty is a black woman, dancing in the fields,
pressing a wind blown rose to her cheek,
while the magnolia sun lights up her face.

Beauty is a fat black woman, smiling at her
child through ivory teeth and shiny indigo eyes,
planting countless kisses, on a tiny curly head.

Alex Branthwaite

THOUGHTS FROM AN INVISIBLE REALITY

Violent sandstorms echo and rebound across the
cold stale tears of a scented flower.
Fields of burning poppies flame across a
barren dying landscape of weeping red
and human sleep.

I yearn to the winds of knowledge and life
for travelling visions that manifest from deep
within the mind-collective.
Thus forcing into submission shapes of
formless gods, who reside within the cadges
of confined bondage.

Soft buzzing bumblebee your sweet honey song drowns
out my eyes of invading seaweed. Stroke little girl the exposed
sour teeth of ancient sleeping kings, thus transforming
your whole world into a frozen nuclear winter of snow.

Awake wise dreaming arachnid and slowly weave with
strands of fine silk my mummified body into a jewelled tapestry
of cocooned stillbirth.

Jeffrey Woods

FORGIVE AND FORGET

Bitterness wanes
Priorities change
Too busy to let it hurt
The law's advice
Gave them no choice
Made history seem very curt

To forget and forgive
Live and let live
Is much harder said than done
Let evil dwell
Should be in hell
It seems the villains won

Lots of people
Lots to forget
Loving, not a strong trait
Can we forgive
Can we let live
The world might have a long wait

Mostly we're sad
When things go so bad
But revenge makes matters worse
Turn your cheek
Be strong, and meek
Let love, put the world in reverse

B M Hurll

MASKED COMPANIONS

Today I wear the young and though she sits outside my soul,
her trembling, dancing, cautious threads turn into my veins,
nudging for movement, gasping for new limits and pleading for
tastes of passion, air and touch.
This is the girl who dreams awake and thrashes wildly in her face.

I am still hesitating into bloom,
all wisdom I know I have not but my mask twitches at the sunlight -
glowing and feeling I wriggle with life.
The nightmare - life grows old.

This future may make me yawn, stay asleep for the needs of musts
rather than the need of want.
I shudder at the air, my bones cringing from the years huddle
together shrinking my frame.
I am scared of youth, its power. I have memories of burning wants
in the dark.
A soul of brilliance with a frame to match could
ignite the moon, without that frame and wrinkles of past I have a
heavy load to carry and cannot reach the sun.

These companions tug at each side of me - a hand each,
making me stand in strange air willing it to freeze, I then could burn
in that instant for always - young and supple, expectant and afraid.
Brimming with hope, no notion of disappointment.
Potential is real and life a mission
and a body to match the arms that will come.

One companion I bless and breathe,
the other I ignore in hope she dies before I do

Victoria Waller

SELF-APPOINTED GRACE

Black and white scene projects colourless parade
Performance short lived upon leisure centre dimlit stage
Faced with banishment as image fades, shamefully unkind
Scrutinised sports consistent bind delights closeted minds
Over filled space with trophies and shields out of media reach
Kits washed frequently to brightly attract putrid teacher
Young bodies emotional vampires seek to bleed, renascent feed
Traditional art forms taught sluggishly
Which victims of circumstance inherit with fear then rear
Nature's womb to produce honesty
Rebirth given to those after extensive feat
Humbleness knelt the once as tarnished lips kiss purify feet
Self-appointed grace shows in corroded face
Fits with abusive race
Poetic truth rests its case.

Alan Jones

MY TWO CAR CRASHES

My two car crashes
Ended up in major smashes
No cause, no way
There's nothing to say

So close near death
To lay on a rose bed
To wake up and see
Is a gift to me

Nothing I could do
That happened to two
So lucky I'm here
I didn't shed my last tear

I ask myself why
I was so close to die
Why choose me I ask
It happened so fast

Would it be better if I'm not here
Nothing to feel, nothing to fear
That's all I dream about, is them two
So many years but not so few

There's so much I fear
Knowing the end is near
Now I can see
How short life can really be.

Stephanie Sharp

THE MILLENNIUM

The year 2000 is getting near,
Lots of people living in fear.
The computer bug, it might not come right,
So lots of people will not want to take a flight.
With everyone working hard,
Let's hope everything is in hand.
When 2000 comes to the land
With coaches, cars by galore,
To take us to see a sunset never seen before.
Firework displays around the world
Some might think that the world has come to an end
Instead of a new century
All over the land
With parties and crowds that's for sure.
Let's hope it makes everyone happy
As never before.
But it's one thing we must not forget
It's 2000 years
Since that bright star was lit.

Doreen Day

SURVIVAL

*(Thanks to the late Roland Barthes, the late T S Eliot, HTV de Ijsberg,
Hypoliet, and Nick Nolet)*

These are not my statements, nor are they by me.
This is a residue of existence.
This is a mirror of nothing but the fears,
the appearances, the intimidations, the aggressions
of a nonlivable environment.
Thus, this is a negative residue of
an immediate corruption of the message.
This is the misery of forced coincidences -
this should be the mystery of survival -
Is it?

Xanadu Ofrushdiefame for Forward Press (February 1999)

FIREWORKS

I saw a firework fly high
Boom, boom, boom
Into colourful raindrops in the sky

It fills the sky with beautiful colours
And they make noisy bangs and booms.
Lovely colours and noises too,
I like them very much.
Every night I watch them
It is very good and nice to see them
Every year.

Craig Lowdell (8)

MILLENNIUM

Soon, the world's turning will find
In time's golden space that rich dawn
That brought its precious light for all
To see behind a humble stable door,
A miracle of birth, a gift from God, a
Showering of glory, the world had
Never seen before, nor would again.
Jesus, the Christ, the saviour of mankind.
And we, the rich heirs of his truth
Weep for the sick hearts that faith
Could not move, and know not God,
Who build the golden calf to mammon
Down in Greenwich, too blind to see
The tears of Christ on his
Sacrificial cross.

Huw Parry

DUST

Where does all the dust come from?
In my life it's become a bane.
I polish it off in the morning
And next day it's there again.

When the sun comes out it shows it up
Though I cleaned there yesterday,
I wish some clever inventor
Would find something to keep it away.

The Good Book says we come from dust
And to dust we must return,
But what to do with the dust in between
Is the lesson I have to learn.

If I polish each day for another week
Will my efforts have been in vain?
For if I turn my back when I've done all that
I'm sure it will be there again!

Pauline Anderson

THE AMAZING BRITISH

The French do not like us, they say
Barbarous, obtuse, lazy tobacco lager louts
The Turks did say, we burn our beds to catch a flea
German poet Heinrich Heine defined silence as
Talking to an Englishman
Hungarian, George Mikes, alone he forms a queue
Other countries have sex, English have hot water bottles
Oh me! Oh my! I agree, I did divorce all three,
Our food comes under the hammer too
Boiled cabbage, fast food, mad cow disease
Chops, crisps, pies more chips, fish and peas
Sixty religions, all downed with tea
Yuk, tapioca pudding, diabolical mustard
Porridge with sugar, sausage and custard
Muddy coffee, biscuits and cheese
Oh me! Oh my! Emigrate at sixty-three
The weather is no better, pollution and asthma
Chest diseases, more people suicidal
Depression, desperation, permanent winter
No courtesy, no humour, no manners
Shaw even said Englishman opens mouth
Other Englishmen despise him
Unmusical, unqualified, unenthusiastic
Oh my! Oh my! I'm proud to be British

Iris Williams

TO A RED POPPY

I haven't always bought a poppy, I confess,
But this year I feel different.
Walking out of the supermarket with my trolley full of goods,
I am grateful for my freedom.
There are no snipers behind the tills;
I have petrol in my car
And a home to go to.
I am nearly 60 and I am alive.
Bosnia, Angola, Rwanda, all around the world
We've seen the suffering.
Television newsmen bring into our homes
The horrors of war.
It's not the buildings that I mourn
It's the people -
Orphans and old people -
Afraid and despairing.

I watched the march past the cenotaph.
You could see the military pride and discipline
Still evident in an aged retinue,
Faces of character,
Their numbers diminishing with each Remembrance Day.
A tear came to my eye, we owe them so much.
I pinned my poppy to my lapel with pride.

E Margaret Holmes

PROGRESS

The church bells rang out gladly, loud and long
Calling people to confess their wrong

I was a child:
The day was mild

Yet I sat frozen stiff upon my seat
The coked-up boiler blew out smoke, not heat

Sixty years of worship have passed; now
Children's, children's children sing and bow
Complaint is rife
When winter strikes

But draughts and smoke and cold as in the past
No longer. Oil has come at last
We can sit in comfort, offset chill
There is no need in church, to grumble still

Dolly Harmer

RETIREMENT?

Does the word mean you have nothing to do,
When your working days are through,
That you can fly out to the sun,
Live it up and have some fun.
Enjoy your life in every way,
Doing nothing from day to day?
As a pensioner, and a wife,
Mine is a very different life,
I'm still working, doing the chores,
An unpaid cleaner, here indoors.
I would far rather go out to work,
Whatever the job, I'd never shirk.
Meeting people, having a natter,
How wonderful to hear some chatter.
Retirement? No it's not for me,
For I'm as fed up as I can be.
For I could go back to work today,
I would be happy in every way,
Because of my age, unfortunately,
I had to retire gracefully.

Penny Rose

THE BEAUTIFUL MAIDEN

She awakes with the early dawn
Exotic is her graceful form
The animals listen to her sing
And she runs and dances
Playfully twirling around with the wind
Known by all the creatures living there
This beautiful maiden with long silky hair
On tiptoes amongst the bluebells
Still wet from morning dew
Exquisite like a butterfly
Skipping her way through
Running swiftly along
Comes her friend
The bob-tailed rabbit, called Bright Eyes
Whilst high up above them
The birds greet her with their cry
She sits to rest against a tree
Quickly the red squirrel races down
To settle there upon her knee
Gently she strokes his bushy tail
And tickles the rabbit's nose
Before walking through the woodland glade
Down to where the river flows
Passing the mouse she calls Morris
The woodland nymph
A legend by knowledge
She is, the goddess of the forest.

Joan Taylor

ODD FELLOWS

When God made us creatures, do you think he got it right?
For he made some black, some yellow, and others just plain white
Did he have a reason? Of this I am not quite sure
For he did not stop at just a few, but is making more and more
If only he had made one colour, and made the same for one and all
And even made the height the same, not some short, some tall
For if we were all one colour, as well as the same height
Then perhaps we would not argue, over who was black or white
The Lord may not have planned it, but it is so, and this I say
It is the cause of all the trouble, in this world today.

S C Wiggins

THE DERELICT

Her sails unfurled and hanging limp, untrimmed,
A tattered hulk, from cardboard berth she crept;
Beneath the railway arches she had slept.
Her bell was badly cracked, her lamps were dimmed.
Not fully crewed, she drifted down the street,
Her pilot in a fog and unaware
Of others passing by or anchored there;
Her only thought to get something to eat.
The smell of bacon wafted, nostrils flared;
The coffee stall hove slowly into view.
If only she could hail someone who cared,
Someone who'd slip her just a bob or two;
Then she could run for shelter from the cold,
Placate the pangs of hunger in her hold.

Frederick Coates

As Shadows Lengthen

Gone now the heat of the day
And before the cool breath of night,
Is a time for quiet contemplation
As shadows lengthen in soft subdued light.
The rough edges that have chafed my spirit
Throughout a tiring day
Are smoothed, as shadows lengthen.
And to myself I say.
It wasn't a bad day after all
Things look better out of the glare of the sun.
In fact I've made new friends today,
Meeting them again will be quite fun.
I sit, as shadows lengthen
And think of the things I have done.
Not great things - but I made someone happy
When I enquired about her son
I look from my chair in the twilight
My old dutch sitting quietly there
No need for words - we've been together so long.
As shadows lengthen - we've peace beyond compare.

Irene Spencer

THE BARGAIN

I brought a car in Spain
It really was a bargain
I had to ship it in
It came via Copenhagen
When I left Dover
We were speeding I admit
But the policeman who pulled me over
Did seem pretty thick
He came alongside the car
We wound the window down
He inserted his head inside
And gave quite a frown
He said, 'Can I see your licence?'
'I've not got one' came the reply
'What about insurance without that you cannot drive?'
I explained 'I've not got any
But before this goes too far
I'm just the passenger
It's a left-hand drive car.'

Steve George

FEELING AS OLD AS CAN BE . . .

Are you feeling as old
As old can be
Has your body travelled south,
Your forehead level with your mouth?

Are you feeling old
As old as old can be
Do you look like you belong on the moon
Wrinkles all over like a prune?

Are you feeling old
As old as old can be
Has all your pulling-power gone
Do you think life's just a con?

Maybe you are old
As old as old can be
But you're only as old as you look
So I bet you wished to look like me!

Vikki George

WHAT IS A BIRTHDAY?

A birthday is something to wish for,
or forget as soon as it came.
To a child it's a doll or a teddy,
when it's older, computer games.
It could be a trip or an outing,
a run down the pub or a show,
to lovers, the back row at the movies,
for the old, just one year to go.

But mostly it's just a reminder,
of things that have past in your life.
To a wife, when her husband forgot one,
to a husband a row with his wife . . .
A memory of a day full of laughter,
or perhaps, a night filled with tears.
The joy of seeing one's first born,
and watching them grow through the years.

But whatever has been the occasion,
be it funny or sad on the day.
It means you will be one year older,
that's something that won't go away.
So do not let that thought bring sorrow,
a birthday's coming, as long as you live.
As long as you have someone to share it,
and return any love that you give.

Geoff Hume

SIGNS

Signs, marks and symbols ever used as a gateway
Or a key to the door, hiding a new pathway.
Each section of life has its own sign, thoughts
Or conjecture, a string of good sense,
Reasoning from ancient observation,
Tuned and tried - and all recalled by a mark.
Such a mark can trigger a creative potential
By probing the unconscious for an answer.
The signs have character to probe deep,
Think out what the message conveys.
A door opens to a realm of archetypes
Lying deep in the unconscious mind -
A creative potential.
A simple mark; a simple sign, a symbol.
To those who cannot see, it's naught;
Hard to detect signal from noise.
To seem, to know, to listen, to find
Is to see life as God ever sees.
Man judges the deed - God the intention.
Life is not as it seems. Real life is hidden.

H Cotterill

FAREWELL

I'm sure that little creature knew
I'd saved her life that day,
When rescued from the leaping cat
Who thought it only play.

Her body gleaming blue and green,
Her wings of gauze outspread,
She stood upright upon my thumb
All fear, it seems, had fled.

She looked at me with those big eyes
And when at last she rose,
She fluttered all around my face,
Brushed cheeks, and lips, and nose.

A magic mem'ry now I hold
As I fell beneath her spell.
I treasure every moment
Of that dragonfly's farewell.

Eddie Merlin

OUR TROUBLES

I've lived in Ulster all my life and am very proud to be,
A man with Northern Ireland blood, yes that's my history,
Now sad to say for thirty years, these years they have been rough,
Much innocent blood it has been shed, for many it has been tough.

I don't know what's behind it all, how man could be so cruel,
To take one's life without a thought, I ask you, is it real?
There's wives and children left to mourn, and brothers and sisters too,
There's mums and dads, there's uncles and aunts, there's many and not
a few.

As loved ones are left to do their grieving, they're shattered no doubt to
the core,
As they mourn the loss of their loved one, well it's something they'll
never get o'er,
Now friends I wish to remind you, that God has said in His Word,
That vengeance is mine and that I will repay, yes these are the Words of
the Lord.

There are many who bomb and are shooting, and causing innocent
blood to be shed,
They feel they are justified in their doings, as for a cause they say they
are led,
But unless they repent as a sinner, and call upon God to forgive,
In Hell they will suffer forever, for their deeds upon earth they did live.

And so ends my poem on 'Our Troubles', in old Ulster that I love
oh so well,
I too am a victim of the gunman, but God spared me I'm glad I can tell,
A bullet was meant to remove me, although injured yet my life God
did spare,
To preach to others about my Saviour, if forgiven His Heaven they
could share.

And so in our land with its troubles, and especially not knowing
what's ahead,
I'm glad that I know Him as Saviour, as by His hand I am safely led,
He will led me and guide me as promised, as we read in His holy Word,
Then afterwards receive me to glory, to be at Home with my
wonderful Lord.

Sydney Ward

PHOTOGRAPHS

Photographs are memories
Of our lives as we have grown;
Bringing back those treasured memories
Of special times that we have known.

First of all our families
The ones we hold so dear;
Of those who are sadly departed
And those still living near.

Followed by the holidays
And places we have seen;
Looking at those photographs
Helps us to remember where we've been.

Then those of friends so far away
Who mean so much to you;
Who share the pictures of their lives
And everything they do.

The ones of places of history
And those of the countryside;
People, places, pets and views
The range it is so wide.

Oh what a joy to recall those times
Of everyone and place we've known;
Each with a special moment
A treasured memory of their own.

Ann Forshaw

TIME

As time goes by on golden wings
Time to remember little things
The tiny thoughts that stay in mind
The vast expanse of all mankind
The tapestry of life we weave
Becomes a goal we must achieve
Because in all the throws of time
We must embrace the sweet divine
But when my time on earth is through
I'd like to spend eternity with you
You did sustain me through our life
I still remain your loving wife

Mary Tickle

MY DOG

My dog is old - I love him so.
I find it hard to let him go.
He sleeps beneath my bed each night.
His gentle snores give me delight.
I smile and then before I know
the rising sun calls out 'Hallo.'
Today I'm up; but he is slow
to find his feet - he doesn't quite.
My dog is old.

I do not cry - but teardrops flow
on, on to reach my chin below.
I'm grieved to see his sorry plight
and ease him up to standing height,
he tries so hard to walk and go.
My dog is old.

Evelyn Golding

THE LAST CHANCE

I've given up trying to help you
there's no more I can do
You've got to stop gambling
or our marriage will be through

I've always had to scrimp and scrape
so we can make ends meet
You should get your act together
stop always trying to cheat

We have three lovely children
and you gamble every day
when they break up from school
we can't afford to go away

I'm giving you one last chance
but you have to make amends
so now it's down to you, whether
our marriage survives or ends.

A Whyte

TYRANNY

Tyrannical regimé and democratic rule
One bearing hate and the other casting doubt
Animals in control and egos being controlled
Threats to avoid and ideas to escape from

Deadly war gases from laboratory games
The mad, sane souls
Breeding lots of pain
The mad, sane parents
Blackening their progeny
The mad, sane killers
Will strike the unlucky few

Licensed torture time
Permitted drug intake
Do the body worship
And spirit denigration

The news all this week
A shocking murder trial
The normal point their fingers
But betray and maltreat
The future adult being

Licensed torture time
Permitted drug intake
Do the body worship
And spirit denigration.

James Rouse

MY SON

Can words convey the special way a mum thinks of a son
Altho' not mine - blood of blood - bone of bone
There couldn't be more caring, than if one of my own
A motherless child I fear from a most tender year
with only a dad and brothers to upbring him
The youngest of four with no mum to restore -
a cherished and a loving feeling
He doesn't complain or a relationship strain
by acting the part of a lout - in fact so easy going
and affable is he - his aggression amounts
To a great deal of nowt!

So here's to our friendship - that's second to none -
With my love to you for being a son.

Margaret M Munton

LEAVING CEREMONY

Peter rushed up to the door.
'I'm off, then!' he cried. 'Finally!'
Suitcases, stuffed, crammed the floor,
Boxes fell, untidily.

'I'm off, then!' he cried. 'Finally!'
'Cheerio!' we replied, once again.
Boxes fell, untidily,
And we thought that he might miss the train.

'Cheerio!' we replied, once again.
We were waiting to kiss him farewell,
And we thought that he might miss the train -
When the cab driver rang at the bell!

We were waiting to kiss him farewell
While he looked for his coat and his hat.
When the cab driver rang at the bell,
There wasn't the time for all that.

While he looked for his coat and his hat,
(Suitcases, stuffed, crammed the floor)
There wasn't the time for all that -
So Peter just rushed out the door.

Penelope Alexander

PLAYING SOLDIERS

Fighting on a battlefield,
War, destruction, hate,
Looking down on the past,
I look at the bloodied state.

You've shattered dreams, shattered promises,
Alone you're wives will die,
Are your memories of your children?
Are they of your wives?
Dead, dank, disfigured as they lie.

Playing games of childhood war,
The deaths that you now hold,
'A game it is, a bit of fun,'
In the past as you were told.

The Jerries, the Jerries, they are the wrong.'
But are they all the same,
Through death you'll never find out as they lie,
A grave without name.

Jemma Bowater

BREAKTHROUGH

The loneliness scattered for all to see
Suffocation for all that lives
The dull cry from strangers who try to push through
Escaping the dark though there is no light

Months of waiting
Handcuffed to the ground
Lonely and scared as their eyes firmly shut
A pain in their head as the earth starts to crumble
A ray of light leading the newborn path

Still cold, still cold
So weak and alone
Can't breathe, don't know how, experience is new
Breakthrough little flower your beauty is bold
Join hands with nature as the sun is now gold

Jennifer Lawson

MY DREAM

In my dream of you
I am sat in a room
Cold and alone
With a feeling of gloom,
The door it then opened
And in you came
I had to pinch myself
Again and again.

You came to my side
You took hold of my hand
All I could hear now
Was the sound of your band,
I was there beside you ever so close
You now looking at me
Handing me a rose.

You were singing a love song
With your tender voice
I just could not move
I had no other choice,
But to keep on looking into
Your blue eyes so deep
Praying no one would wake me
From my most beautiful sleep.

You suddenly stopped singing
Then you did this
Put your lips to mine for
The most wonderful kiss,
Then my dream of you it was gone
I awoke alone in my room
But my dream of you left me
Feeling over the moon.

Angie Stevens

NATURE'S SECRET

Whales, dolphins, catfish galore,
Kingfishers, seagulls, blackbird, macaw.
Peacock, ostrich, non flying birds,
Sheep, goat, buffalo herds.
Tiger, puma, flesh eating cats,
Small furry winged things you'd think were bats.
The cobra, the rattle snake, the venomous ones,
Have mouths as big as a cavern,
And make little rodents run.
The secret to nature will leave you in awe,
And leave you seeking more.

Jay Smoldon (9)

A SPECIAL PET

Swingy, swingy this way, swingy, swingy that,
The family decided to have a pet and didn't want a cat.
Swingy, swingy this way, swingy, swingy that,
A dog mum thought, yes good idea but all he would do - stay sat!
Swingy, swingy this way, swingy, swingy that,
'Get a hamster,' said dad one day, but it looked more like a rat.
Swingy, swingy this way, swingy, swingy that,
At all odds the kids fed up looked at the empty mat.
Swingy, swingy this way, swingy, swingy that,
Uncle Fred fresh from his hols called round with Auntie Pat.
Swingy, swingy this way, swingy, swingy that,
Uncle Fred he'd brought a gift, but why was the box so fat?
Swingy, swingy this way, swingy, swingy that,
He'd brought us a monkey a long armed one, how kind of him and Pat.
Swingy, swingy this way, swingy, swingy that,
He's here, here's there, he's in our hair but we'll never send him back.

Jason Smoldon

CITY AT NIGHT

The bright moon takes its position in the clear sky of the night,
A light breeze rolls in from the sea,
And in the reflection of the moon, tall dark figures stretch out over the
city, touching the horizon.
In the centre of the city neon lights jump out on walls of extreme height,
And silence rules over the city of shadows, excluding the occasional
rustle of leaves,
And maybe the slight whistling of the wind,
As I take this wonderful view into my mind I settle down to sleep,
To take in the colour and excitement of the great outside,
I know my two companions will be doing the same.
I dream there are logs in a heap,
The silence ceases to abide.
An open fire jumps before me, and ashes fall like rain,
The temperature increases along with the flames.
But wait, I am awake, the fire, it is real,
My friends they have left and gone,
'Robert, James.'
The fire thrusts forward, I feel, I feel,
The heat; so strong.
Finally, I'm out in the open, to be greeted by James.
We are safe from danger,
But what of Rob?
. . . There were three in the flames,
Leigh, Rob and James,
But only two remained the same.

Leigh Smoldon (13)

THE ANGEL'S FACE

Mother tucks me in and says 'Goodnight,
The angels won't let the bedbugs bite.
Have no fear.'
I lie awake, afraid to sleep.
I know that no angels keep
A watch here.

Where are the angels? They're meant to be
Here to watch over you and me.
When, oh when, will I ever see
The Angel's Face?

I prickle up. There's steps on the stairs.
Where are they going? Please anywhere
But my room.
I hear them stop. Is it to me they creep?
Will it be a night of wakeful sleep
Or just doom?

Where are the angels? They're meant to be
Here to watch over you and me.
When, oh when, will I ever see
The Angel's Face?

He says it's love that makes him do this,
Yet I feel sick at his touch or kiss.

What's the matter with me?

P Shotter

THE MILLENNIUM

What do I want from the millennium year?
A world that's at peace with no bullet to fear
A world where each Christian, Muslim and Jew
Buddhist and Hindu to name but a few
Will all live together with love for each other
For all religions teach love each man like your brother
Where the tyrants of this world will all go away
Like the Hitlers and Pol Pots of yesterday
A world where each creature of land, sea or air
Will not be pursued for the fur that they wear
The horns on their face or this thing we call sport
Where we slaughter and maim without reason or thought
Stop chemical waste and the burning of trees
Nuclear bombs and the pollution of seas
No more should the rockets hurtle up into space
Costing billions of dollars, what a terrible waste
The money could be used to search for a better way
Of protecting the people keeping starvation at bay
If our leaders and governments try to get these things done
We might have a better world in 2001

Barbara Russell

DAWN OVER THE ATLANTIC

The sun's first rays soft kissed the sky,
Where day and darkness meet;
It glinted on the aircraft's wing
At thirty thousand feet.

It pulled aside earth's starry shroud
As it battled with the night;
It shone below on filmy cloud
As the stars were put to flight.

The night was sped, with leaden tread,
Into its western cave;
As the sun arose from nature's bed,
Reflected on the ocean's waves.

The sparkling shafts of gold display
Earth's marvellous morning story;
The miracle of each new day,
Revealed in all its glory.

In triumph each emerging ray
Heralded day's birth;
The sunset fires of yesterday
Had circled all the earth.

This magical glimpse of divine insight,
On memory leaves implanted,
The wonder of God's natural truths,
And what we take for granted.

John Sanders

THE HOMILY

When life is bleak
And you feel you can't cope
Remember these words
Where there's life, there is hope
You may be alone
And have no one to care
The world owes you nothing
Life can be so unfair
Don't throw life away
Grit your teeth and hang on
You'll find out one day
That self pity is wrong
You were born on this planet
To this wonderful world
Could you miss seeing sunsets
Or a rose just unfurled
And the sound of birds singing
When the sun's shining bright
The moon painting silver
The seashore at night
You are part of this picture
Don't step out of the frame
You have much to live for
There is so much to gain
These wonders of nature
Are there for you free
Don't let it escape you
Use your vision and see
And though you can't see it
You are part of a plan
Unique and important
In the history of man

June Davies

ATTITUDE

You sit there,
angelic angel,
your face innocent,
your mind full of evil,
your white clothes of purity
but your wings are tarnished.
Your life consists of you,
your thoughts,
your needs.
You love you,
you hate us
but you're a nobody,
a nothing,
just a pathetic insect,
you eat away our world of questions.
Your foolish games of attitudes,
is your existence of your foolish life,
for you are a fictitious figure of a human.

Rebecca Breeze

IRAQ CHRISTMAS 1998

To show aggression doesn't pay
We must prove just what we say
And do some friendly bombing
                    Over there.

We must make the right decision
To drop with great precision
Our wonderful cruise missiles
                    Over there.

So we went and passed a motion
Sent our troops across the ocean
And bombed innocent civilians
                    Over there.

And although the missiles missed us
There's no peace on earth for Christmas
May the Good Lord forgive you
                    Mr Blair.

B C Watts

SUBMISSIONS INVITED
SOMETHING FOR EVERYONE

ANCHOR BOOKS '99 - Any subject,
light-hearted clean fun, nothing unprintable
please.

WOMENSWORDS '99 - Strictly women,
have your say the female way!

STRONGWORDS '99 - Warning!
Age restriction, must be between 16-24,
opinionated and have strong views.
(Not for the faint-hearted)

All poems no longer than 30 lines.
Always welcome! No fee!
Cash Prizes to be won!

Mark your envelope (eg *Poetry Now*) **'99**
Send to:
Forward Press Ltd
Remus House, Coltsfood Drive
Woodston, Peterborough, PE2 9JX

**OVER £10,000 POETRY PRIZES
TO BE WON!**

Judging will take place in October 1999